LAUGH-OUT-LOUD JOKES

LAUGH-OUT-LOUD DINOSAUR JOKES

CAITIE MCANENEY

WINDMILL BOOKS

Published in 2025 by Windmill Books, an Imprint of Rosen Publishing
2544 Clinton St., Buffalo, NY 14224

First Edition

Editor: Caitie McAneney
Book Design: Claire Zimmermann

Photo Credits: Cover, p. 1 (child) Q88/Shutterstock.com; series art (dinosaur illustrations) Nadzin/Shutterstock.com, (paper texture) OanaGherghe2/Shutterstock.com; p. 5 Dotted Yeti/Shutterstock.com; p. 7 Warpaint/Shutterstock.com; p. 9 Alberto Andrei Rosu/Shutterstock.com; p. 11 CSA Images/iStock; p. 13 Dariush M/Shutterstock.com; p. 15 Orla/Shutterstock.com; p. 17 DM7/Shutterstock.com; pp. 18, 20 (illustrations) Panda Vector/Shutterstock.com; p. 19 Rafael Trafaniuc/Shutterstock.com; p. 21 Gorodenkoff/Shutterstock.com.

Library of Congress Cataloging-in-Publication Data

Names: McAneney, Caitie, author.
Title: Laugh-out-loud dinosaur jokes / Caitie McAneney.
Description: Buffalo : Windmill Books, 2025. | Series: Laugh-out-loud jokes | Includes index.
Identifiers: LCCN 2024005114 (print) | LCCN 2024005115 (ebook) | ISBN 9781538396742 (library binding) | ISBN 9781538396735 (paperback) | ISBN 9781538396759 (ebook)
Subjects: LCSH: Dinosaurs–Juvenile humor.
Classification: LCC PN6231.D65 M33 2024 (print) | LCC PN6231.D65 (ebook) | DDC 818/.6020803625679–dc23/eng/20240214
LC record available at https://lccn.loc.gov/2024005114
LC ebook record available at https://lccn.loc.gov/2024005115

Manufactured in the United States of America

CPSIA Compliance Information: Batch #CSWM25. For further information, contact Rosen Publishing at 1-800-237-9932

CONTENTS

Dino Days 4
Dinos on the Move! 6
On the Job 8
At Home 10
Frights and Bites 12
In the Mix 14
Dino School 16
Gross! 18
Fun with Fossils 20
Glossary 22
For More Information 23
Index 24

Words in the glossary appear in **bold** the first time they are used in the text.

DINO DAYS

Why did *Archaeopteryx* catch the worm?

SHE WAS AN EARLY BIRD!

What is a dinosaur's favorite breakfast?

TYRANNOSAURUS CHEX!

Are baby dinosaurs cute?

YES, THEY'RE A-ROAR-ABLE!

What does *T. Rex* do at night?

DINO-SNORE.

FUN FACT!

Archaeopteryx is considered one of the earliest birds on Earth. It was a small, bird-like dinosaur that lived in the Late **Jurassic** Period.

DINOS ON THE MOVE!

What did *Triceratops* fall on?

HIS TRICERA-BOTTOM.

What game can *Brontosaurus* play?

SQUASH.

Why is *Stegosaurus* so great at volleyball?

SHE CAN REALLY SPIKE!

How do you know who is winning a game of dinosaur basketball?

CHECK THE DINO-SCORE.

FUN FACT!

Stegosaurus was a large, plant-eating dinosaur. It had bony plates down its back and a powerful spiked tail.

ON THE JOB

Was the dinosaur comedian funny?

YES, HE WAS DINO-MITE!

What kind of dinosaur makes a good police officer?

TRICERA-COPS.

Why did the doctor give *T. Rex* a Band-Aid?

HE HAD A DINO-SORE.

Why do dinosaurs make good authors?

THEY HAVE LONG TALES.

FUN FACT!

Triceratops had one of the largest skulls of any land animal ever known. It had three horns and a large **frill**.

AT HOME

What do dinosaurs use for their kitchen floor?

REP-TILES.

How did the paleontologist fix his house?

HE USED A DINO-SAW.

Where did *Brontosaurus* shop for groceries?

THE DINO-STORE.

Could dinosaurs jump higher than a house?

OF COURSE THEY COULD. HOUSES CAN'T JUMP!

FUN FACT!

Brontosaurus was a large, plant-eating dinosaur with a long tail and neck. Its name means "thunder lizard" in Greek.

FRIGHTS AND BITES

What do you get when you cross a witch and a dinosaur?

A DINO-SORCERER.

What do you call a prehistoric ghost?

A SCARE-O-DACTYL!

What do you get when you cross a snowman with a dinosaur?

FROSTBITE.

What was the scariest creature to ever fly?

THE TERROR-DACTYL.

FUN FACT!

Pterodactylus was a large, flying reptile. It belonged to a group called pterosaurs and is sometimes called a pterodactyl.

IN THE MIX

What happens if you mix a pig and T. Rex?

JURASSIC PORK.

What do you get when you mix cheese with a dinosaur?

GORGON-ZILLA.

What do you get when you mix a frog with a dinosaur?

TRICERA-HOPS.

What do you get when you mix a horse and a dinosaur?

BRONCO-SAURUS.

FUN FACT!

The Jurassic Period lasted from around 200 million to 145 million years ago. It was called a "golden time for dinosaurs."

DINO SCHOOL

What do you call a dinosaur with a big **vocabulary**?

A THESAURUS!

How did the dinosaur feel on her first day of school?

SHE WAS A NERVOUS REX!

Why didn't the dinosaur give up?

SHE WAS A TRY-CERATOPS.

Why did the *T. Rex* students fall asleep?

THEIR TEACHER WAS A DINO-BORE.

FUN FACT!

Tyrannosaurus Rex, also known as T. Rex, was a fearsome hunter. This meat eater had 60 huge teeth to crush its **prey.**

GROSS!

What do you call a *Stegosaurus* who needs a bath?

A STINK-O-SAURUS.

Why can't you hear *Pterodactylus* go to the bathroom?

BECAUSE THE P IS SILENT!

What do you call a dinosaur with gas?

A BLAST FROM THE PAST!

Did all the smelly dinosaurs die out?

YES, THEY'RE EX-STINKED.

FUN FACT!

Dinosaurs lived on Earth for about 165 million years! About 65 million years ago, they went **extinct**.

FUN WITH FOSSILS

Can pirates be paleontologists?

NO, THEY ARE ARRR-CHAELOGISTS.

What do you call fossils that have been sitting around for millions of years?

LAZY BONES.

Why did the paleontologist get upset?

HE HAD A BONE TO PICK.

Why did the paleontologist want to keep his fossil?

IT HAD SEDIMENTAL VALUE.

FUN FACT!

Archaeologists study things people left behind in the past. Paleontologists study fossils that can be found in **sedimentary rock.**

GLOSSARY

extinct: No longer existing.

frill: The part of an animal that sticks out around its head or neck.

Jurassic: Having to do with the time period from about 180 million to 135 million years ago.

paleontologist: A scientist who studies the past using fossils.

prey: An animal hunted by other animals for food.

sedimentary rock: The rock that forms when sand, stones, and other matter are pressed together over a long time.

sorcerer: Someone who does magic.

thesaurus: A book that lists words along with other words that are like and unlike them.

vocabulary: The words someone knows.

FOR MORE INFORMATION

BOOKS

Brink, Tracy Vonder. *The Tyrannosaurus Rex.* St. Catharines, ON: Crabtree Publishing, 2024

Derrick, Stevie, Dean R. Lomax, and John Woodward. *1,000 Amazing Dinosaur Facts.* New York, NY: DK Publishing, 2023.

Gerry, Lisa M. *Big Words for Little Paleontologists.* Washington, DC: National Geographic, 2023.

WEBSITES

Dinosaurs
kids.nationalgeographic.com/animals/prehistoric
Click on different dinosaur pictures to learn more about each one.

Tyrannosaurus Rex
kids.britannica.com/kids/article/Tyrannosaurus-Rex/353881
Explore more fun facts about *Tyrannosaurus Rex*!

INDEX

archaeologists, 20, 21

Archaeopteryx, 4, 5

birds, 4, 5

Brontosaurus, 6, 10, 11, 14

extinct, 19

fossils, 20, 21

Greek, 11

hunter, 17

Jurassic Park, 14

Jurassic Period, 15

Stegosaurus, 6, 7, 18

paleontologist ,10, 20

prey, 17

Pterodactylus, 12, 13, 18

sedimentary rock, 20, 21

skulls, 9

Triceratops, 6, 8, 9, 14, 16

Tyrannosaurus Rex, 4, 8, 14, 16, 17